KU-092-302

{geography focus}

RUNNING WATER

{our most precious resource}

Louise Spilsbury

www.raintreepublishers.co.uk
Visit our website to find out more information about **Raintree** books.

To order:
☎ Phone 44 (0) 1865 888112
🖹 Send a fax to 44 (0) 1865 314091
🖥 Visit the Raintree Bookshop at **www.raintreepublishers.co.uk** to browse our
catalogue and order online.

First published 2006 by Heinemann Library a division of
Harcourt Education Australia, 20 Thackray Road, Port Melbourne
Victoria 3207 Australia (a division of Reed International Books
Australia Pty Ltd, ABN 70 001 002 357). Visit the Heinemann
Library website at www.heinemannlibrary.com.au

Published in Great Britain in 2006 by Raintree, Halley Court,
Jordan Hill, Oxford OX2 8EJ, part of Harcourt Education
www.raintreepublishers.co.uk

 A Reed Elsevier company

© Reed International Books Australia Pty Ltd 2006

10 09 08 07 06
10 9 8 7 6 5 4 3 2 1

All rights reserved. No part of this publication may be reproduced,
stored in a retrieval system or transmitted in any form or by any means
(electronic, mechanical, photocopying, recording or otherwise) without
the prior written permission of the publisher.

Editorial: Moira Anderson, Carmel Heron, Diyan Leake, Patrick Catel
Cover, text design & graphs: Marta White
Photo research: Karen Forsythe, Wendy Duncan
Production: Tracey Jarrett, Duncan Gilbert
Map diagrams: Guy Holt
Technical diagrams: Nives Porcellato & Andy Craig

Typeset in 12/17.5 pt Gill Sans Regular
Origination by Modern Age
Printed and bound in Hong Kong, China by South China
Printing Company Ltd

The paper used to print this book comes from sustainable resources.

National Library of Australia Cataloguing-in-Publication data:

Spilsbury, Louise.
   Running water : our most precious resource.

   Includes index.
   For upper primary and lower secondary school students.
   ISBN 1 74070 276 X.

   1. Water – Juvenile literature. 2. Water-supply – Juvenile
   literature. I. Title. (Series : Spilsbury, Louise. Geography focus).

553.7

Acknowledgements

The publisher would like to thank the following for permission to
reproduce copyright material: AAP Image/Gavin Lower: p. **16**; APL/
Corbis/Sergio Dorantes: p. **18**, /Ecoscene: p. **19**, /Michael Freeman:
p. **14**, /Danny Lehman: p. **21**, /Minden Pictures/Flip Nicklin: p. **38**,
/Premium Stock: p. **22**, /Steven Starr: p. **29**; Corbis Royalty Free Images:
pp. **8, 42**; Ecoscene/Alexandra Elliott Jones: p. **37**; Getty Images/AFP/
Alessandro Abbonizio: p. **23**, /Aurora/Peter Essick: p. **20**, /National
Geographic Society: p. **33** (lower); GlobeXpress: p. **9**; Dennis Hoffman:
p. **41**; Lonely Planet Images/Claver Carroll: p. **34**, /Richard I'Anson,
p. **24**; Newspix: p. **33** (upper); Photolibrary.com: p. **10**, /Age
Fotostock: p. **36**, /Peter Arnold Images Inc., p. **30**; Still Pictures/Ron
Giling: p. **4**, /Gil Moti: p. **43**, /Jorgen Schytte: p. **12**, /Paul Springett:
p. **11**. All other images PhotoDisc.

Cover photograph of mountain stream and inset image of polluted river
reproduced with permission of PhotoDisc.

Every attempt has been made to trace and acknowledge copyright.
Where an attempt has been unsuccessful, the publisher would be
pleased to hear from the copyright owner so any omission or error
can be rectified.

Disclaimer

All the Internet addresses (URLs) given in this book were valid at the
time of going to press. However, due to the dynamic nature of the
Internet, some addresses may have changed, or sites may have changed
or ceased to exist since publication. While the author and publishers
regret any inconvenience this may cause readers, no responsibility
for any such changes can be accepted by either the author or
the publishers.

DUDLEY PUBLIC LIBRARIES

L

675252   SCH

J 546.22

{contents}

Words that are printed in bold, **like this**, are explained in the Glossary on page 46.

{the world's water}

Earth is known as the 'blue planet' because water covers almost three-quarters of its surface. Nearly all of this water is seawater in seas and oceans. People cannot use seawater. Freshwater from rain and rivers is the water that gives us life and there is only a limited amount of this kind available to us.

Why do we need water?

Almost two-thirds of your body weight is water. Although you can go weeks without food, you would only last a few days without water. Plants also rely on water for life as they use it to make their own food. Almost every **food web** in the world starts with plants. That means that without water we would be very hungry as well as thirsty.

Why can't we drink seawater?

Seawater contains a large amount of salt. If you drank too much of it you would die. The body's cells would dry up as they tried to get rid of all the saltwater. Seawater would kill plants, too, if you watered them with it.

Forget gold, diamonds, or oil – freshwater is the most precious natural resource in the world.

Where is the world's water?

This map shows the amounts of freshwater available to people in different parts of the world. People in some places have much less water than those in other places.

Sometimes there is not enough water in a place because the **climate** is too dry. Climate is the usual weather in a place. Often it is because too many people have to share the available water. For example, less rain falls on Australia than on many parts of Asia. But on average each Australian person has far more water than each Asian person. The reason is that the population of Asia is massively bigger than Australia's. So the water in Asia has to be shared among far more people.

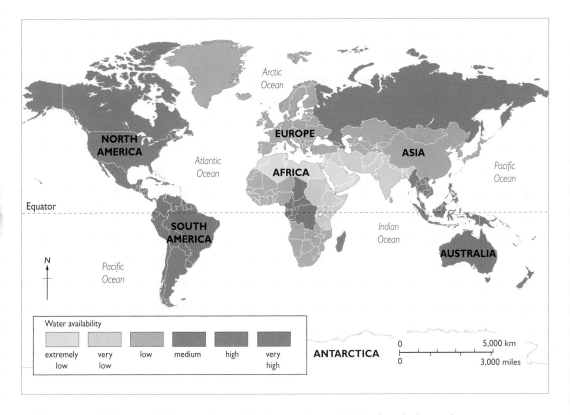

This map of the world shows where freshwater is available: the darker colours show countries that have a high amount of water available for people living there. The lighter colours show countries where people do not have good access to clean freshwater.

{where does water come from?}

The freshwater that people can use is found on and below the surface of our planet. Surface freshwater is the kind found in streams, rivers, lakes, and ponds. Around half of all the water that the people of the world use comes from water supplies like this. The other half comes from what is known as **groundwater** sources.

Groundwater

When rain falls or snow melts on the land, much of this water soaks into the ground. Sometimes it flows into underground streams or forms pools below the ground. Underground water sources like these can take thousands of years to collect. People collect this water from wells or it comes to the surface naturally through springs. We call these water sources **aquifers**.

FACT!

Water is the only thing on Earth to appear naturally in three forms: liquid (water), solid (ice), and gas (**water vapour**).

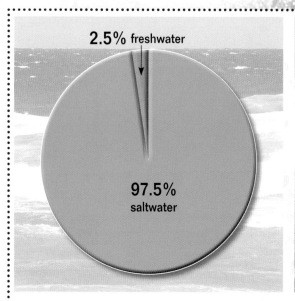

2.5% freshwater

97.5% saltwater

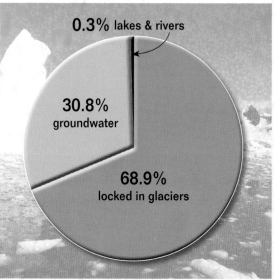

0.3% lakes & rivers

30.8% groundwater

68.9% locked in glaciers

The first pie chart shows us that out of all the water on the planet, only 2.5 percent is freshwater. The second pie chart shows that very little of this drinkable water is in lakes and rivers. Nearly all is frozen in polar ice or hard to get at because it is underground.

The water cycle

There is the same amount of water on and around our planet now as there has been for about 2 billion years. The water that falls when it rains is not extra that we can use. It is part of the **water cycle**. Just as the wheels on a bicycle go around and around, water in the water cycle circulates from the Earth to the sky and back again.

How does it work?

When the Sun heats drops of water at the surface of oceans and rivers, they **evaporate**. This means that they turn into water vapour, an invisible gas in the air. This is what happens when damp washing dries on the line. The water vapour is blown about by the wind and rises in the air. High in the sky it is cold. When the water vapour cools, it turns back into tiny drops of liquid water. This process is called **condensation**. The water then falls back to Earth as rain or, if it is very cold, hail or snow. Then the cycle begins again.

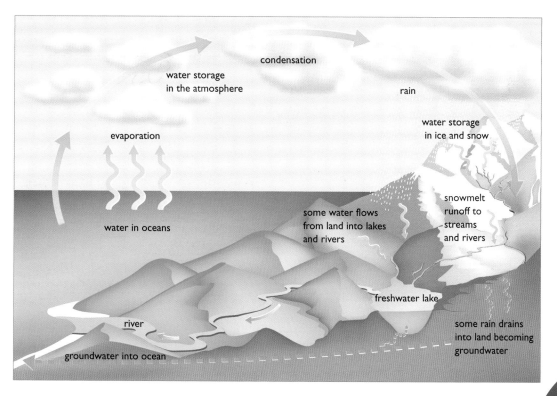

This diagram shows the water cycle.

{how do rivers form?}

Rivers are the most important suppliers of freshwater for most of the people on the planet. The **source**, or start, of a river is usually at the top of mountains and hills. When rain falls and snow melts, they flow down the slopes in streams. As these streams meet, they join and become rivers.

A river's power

When water flows downhill, it gathers speed and force. It rushes over land and washes off loose bits of stone, sand, and soil, which it carries along with it. These bits of **sediment** and rock crash and scrape against the land as the water flows over it. This is a type of **erosion**. Over time, rivers carve out the valleys and channels in the land they flow through.

FACT!

The longest river in the world is the Nile. It is 6,670 kilometres (about 4,100 miles) long. From its source, Lake Victoria in Uganda, it travels north through three countries: Uganda, Sudan, and Egypt.

Fast-moving rivers on steep mountain slopes like this have a lot of cutting power. They can carve straight channels to flow through as they head downhill.

At a river's end

Some rivers flow into natural lakes, into **reservoirs**, or into other rivers. Many rivers flow down onto ever more gently sloping land, all the way to the sea. At the **estuary**, or mouth, of a river where it joins the sea, the water usually flows slowest. This is because the land is flatter here. Then the sediment that was eroded and carried along by the river is dropped or **deposited** on the bottom.

The Nile Delta

This is the Nile Delta, the area where the mighty River Nile meets the sea. A **delta** is the area at the end of a river where loads of sediment have been deposited. From the air, deltas usually look fan-shaped. The banks of sediment in the Nile Delta spread far out to sea. The river breaks up into little rivers that wind their way around all the piles of sediment as they make their way to the sea. People live on deltas because the soil deposited by the river is good for growing **crops** such as rice or cotton.

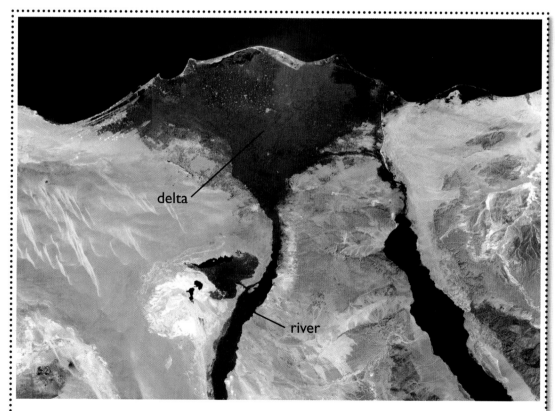

delta

river

This photo provides an aerial view of the Nile Delta.

{lakes, ponds, and wetlands}

Lakes, ponds, and **wetlands** are different from rivers because they are areas of still water, not flowing or running water. However, they are still important supplies of freshwater that are vital for people and for the health of our planet.

Lakes and ponds

Lakes and ponds form where water collects in dips in the land. Some lakes form where rivers are blocked by ice or rock. As the water can go no further it collects together. The running water of the river constantly tops up lakes like this.

FACT!

Reservoirs are artificial lakes. People build them to collect and store water from rivers or rainfall. The water is then ready to pipe to people's homes when they need it.

Lakes are vital suppliers of freshwater. They are also beautiful places we can enjoy for watersports such as boating, swimming, or fishing.

Wetlands and our world

Wetlands are areas of land that are damp and boggy, and often have pools of freshwater lying across their surface. They are often found around rivers, lakes, and streams.

Wetlands are very useful places. The reeds and other plants that grow there mean that wetlands act like sieves. They filter out mud and dirt and improve the quality of the freshwater in the area. Wetlands also work like giant sponges, soaking up water that hits the land suddenly in rainstorms. This allows the rainwater to drain gradually into rivers or into **groundwater** supplies, rather than **flooding** the land.

*Wetlands like this one at the Okavanga **Delta** in Botswana, Africa, are very important places for wildlife. They provide water, food, and shelter for huge numbers of plants and animals.*

{how do people get water?}

For many people around the world, the water in their taps comes from **reservoirs**. Even if reservoir water looks clean, it has mud, dust, and **germs** mixed with it. Before we can use this water it needs to be cleaned or purified. Usually, the water drains through a mixture of sand and gravel to sieve out the dirt. Then chemicals are added to destroy any remaining germs and leave the water clean.

From tank to pipe

The clean water is kept in storage tanks until it is needed. Then it flows through large pipes, buried underground where we cannot see them. These large pipes, called mains, run under the streets to towns and cities. The water flows from these into smaller pipes as it gets closer to buildings. Then it enters even smaller pipes that are attached to the sinks, toilets, baths, and showers in our homes.

People in the wealthier countries of the world simply turn on a tap at home to get the water they need for washing, cooking, or cleaning. However, in many other countries people may have to walk up to three hours a day to fetch water for their families.

Getting and using water

This bar chart shows the different amounts of water used by people who get their water in four different ways. Richer people can get water easily from several different taps or bathrooms in their house. They use a lot more water than poorer people who have to travel to collect their own water. These people may get their water from a tap in their backyard or street. They may have to walk to a pump or stream and carry the water back in containers. Sometimes people in poorer countries have to travel further for water if they have to pay too much for water closer to home.

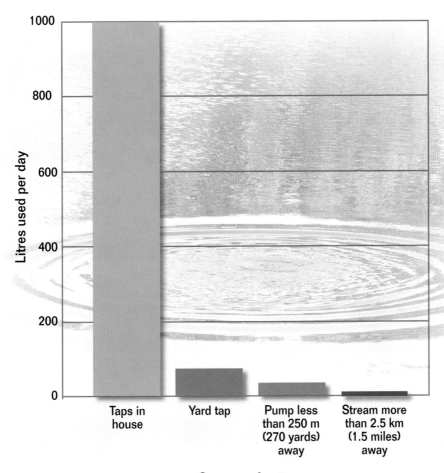

This bar chart shows the amounts of water people use from four different sources.

{how is water used?}

Like all living things, people need water to stay alive. They also use water for a variety of things, some of which you may have never have even thought about.

People in homes, schools, and offices use water for drinking, cooking, cleaning, flushing toilets, and watering gardens. Farmers spray water on their food plants to help them grow. This is called **irrigation**. Factories use water to cool and clean machinery. Water treatment plants also use a lot of water to clean the water that comes to our homes in pipes. Water is even used to make electricity. **Hydroelectric power** stations are places that use the power of falling water to turn wheels called turbines. Special magnets turn this spinning energy into electricity.

FACT!

It takes a vast amount of water to grow food **crops**. It may take 1,000 tonnes (1,100 tons) of water to produce just 1 tonne (1.1 ton) of grain.

People use a lot of water by filling up swimming or paddling pools to cool down in during hot weather. They also use a lot of water on their lawns.

Who uses most water?

Imagine that the total amount of freshwater used by people is like a whole pie. Households, agriculture, and industry use up different shares of the total. The shares can be drawn as different-sized pieces of a pie chart. You can see from the chart that by far the biggest user of water is agriculture. Farmers use almost 70 percent of freshwater to irrigate their crops and fields.

Industries, such as factories and mines, use 22 percent, or almost one-quarter, of the total amount of water people use.

Although households (domestic) use a lot of water, the water that flows down our drains is only 8 percent of the total used.

This pie chart shows the average uses of water across the world. In reality the amount of water taken for different uses varies between countries. A pie chart like this for Africa would look quite different, because farmers there take almost 90 percent of the total water used. A pie chart for Europe would show industry as the biggest user, because it accounts for over half of the water used there.

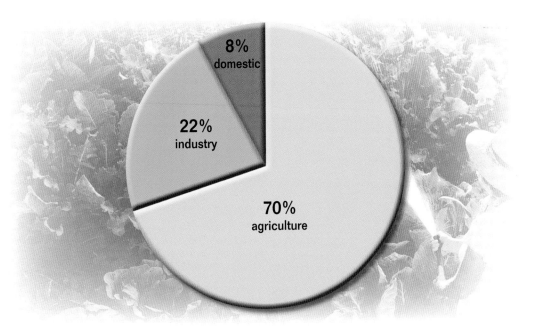

This pie chart shows how water is used around the world.

{the importance of clean water}

Everyone in the world needs to be able to get clean, safe water every day in order to be healthy. When people do not have easy access to clean water, they may have to use dirty water. People can catch diseases by drinking water that is dirty. This is because dirt contains **germs** that can cause disease. Insects such as mosquitoes that breed in dirty water may spread germs when they bite people.

FACT!

- One out of every five people on Earth does not have access to safe drinking water.

- Half the world's people do not have a clean place to go to the toilet or wash themselves.

- Around 25,000 people a day die from drinking dirty water.

In countries that usually have enough water, there may be water shortages in particularly dry weather. This can be a nuisance because people have to limit the amount they use. They may have to buy tankloads of water from elsewhere. However, it is rarely life threatening. In this picture, water from the lorry is filling up the water tank.

Many children miss school because they are sick from drinking dirty water or because they have to walk a long way to collect water for their family. When they miss out on education it means they have less chance of getting work. They may not then earn enough money to feed themselves and their families in the future.

Who needs water?

The total number of people who cannot get safe water regularly is 1.1 billion. More people in Asia and Africa have problems getting clean water than people living anywhere else. Many parts of Africa have **hot climates** with limited rain. South-east Asia, where the greatest populations live, has a short wet season called a **monsoon**, which brings a lot of water, but it comes all at once. It often **erodes** land or causes **floods**. The chart does not include **more developed countries**, where everyone can get clean water.

Cities have **reservoirs** and water pipes to supply water to large numbers of people. People in the country are more spread out, with fewer water pipes to their homes. That is why more people in rural areas (countryside) have unsafe water than those in urban (city) areas.

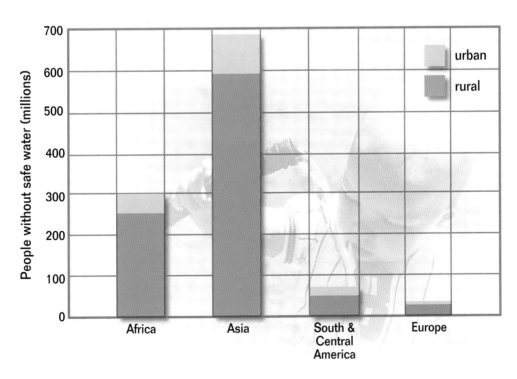

This bar chart shows the people who cannot get access to a safe water supply.

17

{water and population growth}

One of the problems with the world's water is that the world's population is growing fast. There are more and more people on the planet who need to use it. This problem is made worse by the fact that many people today are using much more water than people did in the past. There are only three times more people on the planet today than there were 100 years ago, but our demand for water has increased by six times!

Cities

When a country's population grows, its cities get bigger and bigger as people move into them to find homes and work. This puts a big strain on a city's water supplies. The **sewage** systems are often unable to cope with the human waste from increased numbers of people. This usually means that the poorest people end up without adequate **sanitation**. They may have to use ditches and streams for going to the toilet and washing. This makes the water dirty and leads to disease.

Many richer homes in big cities use vast amounts of water while many people in the poorer parts live without basic sanitation.

Many cities are taking so much water out of their **aquifers** every year that these **groundwater** sources are being sucked dry. The other problem with cities is that large areas of ground are covered with concrete. When rain falls on concrete, it cannot seep into the soil, rivers, or aquifers as it once did.

Trying to meet demand

To provide the people in their countries with water, governments build more **reservoirs** and increase the amounts of water they take from groundwater sources. However, this can lead to more problems. For example, when people dig deeper and deeper in one area to get water, it may wash salts from the underground soil. These salts spoil the freshwater.

This photo shows the groundwater provided by a large aquifer in Arizona, USA. Most of the freshwater available for people to use is found underground in aquifers. It takes hundreds of years for water to trickle in and refill aquifers. People in cities use a lot of water, so their groundwater resources are being used up a lot faster than nature can refill them.

{case study}
the sinking city

Mexico City is one of the biggest and most crowded cities in the world. It has a population of 24 million people, which is nearly one-fifth of Mexico's whole population. The city depends on **groundwater** for 80 percent of its water supply. This water comes from an **aquifer** that is being emptied fast. This is causing the soft, sandy ground in this area – and Mexico City itself – to sink.

Buildings, railways, and roads are collapsing with the soil. A nearby lake is now higher than the sinking city. When heavy rains fall, water in the lake spills over its sides, causing widespread **floods**.

Many fine buildings in Mexico City, like this church, are collapsing as the ground beneath them falls away.

The problem is made worse because a lot of the water pumped from the aquifer is wasted before it even reaches the city. The pipes that supply the water were installed over 100 years ago. Many are broken or cracked. They cannot cope with the increased water demands of the growing city.

What can be done?

The city's government is trying to teach its people to use less water. It is mending leaks and laying new pipes in an effort to reduce the amount of water wasted. It is also looking at ways of catching and storing rainwater that could be piped to homes. Another solution is to make people pay more for their water. When people have to pay for their water they are more careful about how much they use.

FACT!

Mexico City has sunk more than 10 metres (11 yards) in the past 70 years. That is higher than five adult men standing on each other's shoulders. The city is still sinking at a rate of about 30 centimetres (12 inches) a year in some places.

This is an aerial view of Mexico City, one of the largest cities in the world. This giant city and its population are in serious danger of running out of clean water in the future.

{how does water get polluted?}

When water is made dirty or poisonous in some way, we say it is **polluted**. Polluted water can harm or even kill people who use it. Pollution is a serious threat to water supplies all over the world. It is reducing the amount of clean water available to us all.

FACT!

Ninety percent of cities in the **less-developed countries** of the world pump their sewage straight into rivers, lakes, and oceans without treating it (cleaning it) first.

Kinds of pollution

Some water is polluted when **sewage** is pumped into rivers or people drop litter there. Factories sometimes dump poisonous waste chemicals into drains and rivers. Rain can wash oil and grease from roads into water sources. And as rain flows off fields, it can wash **fertilizers** and other chemicals used in farming into rivers or **aquifers**. Some pollution is caused when rainwater mixes with pollution in the air to form **acid rain**. When this **acidic** rain falls into our rivers, it pollutes the water.

Some kinds of water pollution, like this, are easy to see, but even water that looks clean may still be polluted.

Cleaning up

Cities and industries can reduce water pollution by removing harmful substances from waste before pouring those wastes into rivers and lakes. People can help by reducing the amounts of grease, oil, leftover paint, or chemical-rich cleaning fluids that they wash down drains. Many farmers already set aside strips of land to separate fields of **crops** from rivers to reduce the risk of pollution from fertilizers. Governments in many countries are bringing in stricter laws to stop factories and other companies dumping waste in rivers.

The River Thames

The River Thames, which passes through London, is thought to be one of the cleanest rivers in the world. However, it faces pollution problems too. In August 2004, thousands of fish were killed by water pollution caused by sewage that had been spilled into the water. After canoeists complained the water had made them ill, water sports enthusiasts were told to keep off the river until it had been cleaned up.

When sewage was pumped into the River Thames in August 2004, it resulted in polluted water and dead fish in the river. The city's old drainage system could not cope after a spell of heavy rain.

{case study}
Ganges River

The Ganges is the longest river in India. It flows 2,500 kilometres (1,500 miles) from its **source** in the Himalayan Mountains in the north of India to the sea at the Bay of Bengal in Bangladesh. Nearly one-tenth of the world's population live in the land surrounding this great river. The busy towns and industries here dump vast amounts of waste into the Ganges. As well as harming people, this **pollution** also threatens rare kinds of fish, dolphins, and turtles that live and feed in the river.

FACT!

• Around 114 cities along the Ganges dump a total of 1.4 billion tonnes (1.5 million tons) of sewage in the river each day.

• One person in the Ganges River area dies every minute from diarrhoea, a disease caused by drinking polluted water.

Many people in India follow the religion called Hinduism. For them the Ganges is a sacred river and bathing in the holy river water is a vital part of their religion. Unfortunately, when people today bathe in the Ganges, as they are doing here at the city of Varanasi, they risk catching disease.

What pollutes the Ganges?

This map shows the different things that pollute the Ganges River as it flows from source to sea. Check the map key to see what kinds of pollution are caused in different places.

Some pollution comes from waste chemicals dumped by factories that make silk fabric, shoes, **fertilizers**, or medicines.

At leather tanneries, animal skins are made into leather for shoes by being soaked in strong chemicals. The waste chemicals are then dumped in the river.

Dead human and animal bodies rotting in the river cause pollution. When a Hindu dies, the family has the body cremated (burnt) and the remains are placed in the holy Ganges River. Some people cannot afford the cremation, so they simply throw the bodies into the water.

Millions of litres of city waste, including sewage, waste food, and rubbish, pour into the river every day. Treating the **sewage** alone would reduce the pollution in the river by 80 percent.

INDIA

source of the Ganges

CHINA

Delhi

Ganges River

NEPAL

N

Kanpur

Allahabad

Patna

Ganges River

Varanasi

BANGLADESH

INDIA

- city waste
- waste from medicine factories
- waste from fertilizer factories
- waste from leather tanneries
- waste from shoe factories
- waste from Calcutta port
- oil-refining and industrial zone
- dead bodies
- dead animals

Calcutta   Ganges Delta

0   300 km
0   100 miles

Bay of Bengal

This map of the Ganges River shows where most pollution goes into the river.

{water and farming}

Plants need water to grow, whether they are houseplants on a windowsill or **crops** in a field. Across the world, farming uses up vast amounts of freshwater for **irrigation**.

Problems and solutions

One problem with the amount of water used by farming is that much of it is wasted. It drains into the ground before plants can soak it up, so farmers take more and more. In the future sprinkler systems that drip water directly onto the crops should help waste less water. If the land is hot and dry, water is also lost because it **evaporates** from the surface of the soil. One way of avoiding this problem is for farmers to water their crops at night, when it is cooler.

FACT!

It takes an average of 3,450 litres (900 gallons) of water to produce 1 kilogram (2 pounds) of rice.

These huge sprinkler systems are watering fields of wheat in Australia.

Water around the world

Rain does not fall evenly over the Earth. This map shows the average yearly amounts of rainfall across the world. The darkest coloured areas receive the most rain and the palest areas receive the least.

Irrigation water is vital for growing crops in countries that have long periods with little or no rainfall. Even in places that get plenty of rain, irrigated land is still twice as productive as cropland watered only by rainfall. Farmers in dry regions, such as Egypt and south-western USA, would not be able to grow crops without irrigation. Irrigation is also hugely important to farmers in countries such as Australia, which have long spells of **drought**. Irrigation water keeps crops alive when wild plants are dying. In some drier places, farmers are growing crops that require less water to grow. In Israel, farmers are growing a cactus that only needs a small amount of water. It produces an edible fruit, called a kubo, all year round.

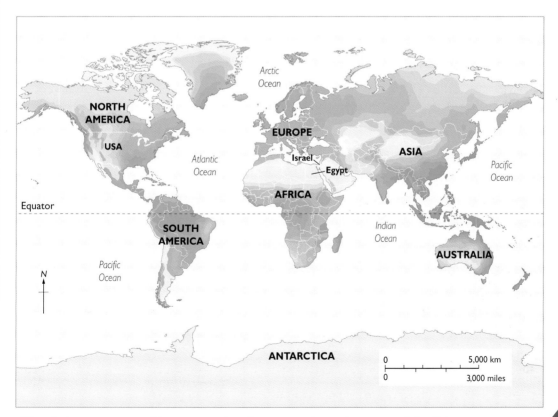

The darkest areas on this map receive the most rain each year, and the lightest areas receive the least.

{land use and water}

People use the land in many different ways. We cover it with concrete and buildings. We dig up coal to burn. We block rivers to collect water for farming and industry. These uses are all important for people's lives. But what effect do they have on the environment and our water supplies?

Dams

People use **dams** to block rivers and collect water in **reservoirs**. They use the water for drinking or **irrigation** and for **hydroelectric power** stations. However, some people are worried that dams affect the way a river's water is shared out. For example, some dams stop water flowing to places where it is needed. This reduces the amount of water available for people living there.

Moving mountains

Around half of the world's people rely on the freshwater that collects on mountains and drains into rivers and the land. This water supply is being affected by people's activities in mountain areas.

Water supplies are affected when forests in mountain regions are cut down. Rain can more easily wash away soil and cause floods in the valleys below.

Some mountain forests are cut to sell wood. Many are cleared so that the land can be used, for example, to build hydroelectric power stations, mines, and the roads, bridges, and tunnels needed to get to these places. The problem is that tree roots hold the soil together and leaves and branches take some of the force of rainfall in a storm. When the land is bare, rain can wash a top layer of soil right down the mountain slopes. When this mud runs into rivers and lakes, it can **pollute** them. Water also may move more quickly down the slope, causing **flooding**. People in the valleys below must drain the precious water, rather than collecting and using it.

Mining

How can mining affect water? Many of the things we use, from pencils to computers, are made from materials dug from the earth in mines. One problem arises with the rocks and rubble that are dug out to create the mines. They are often dumped in low-lying areas, often filling up **wetlands** or other water sources. Also, when certain rocks are dug up, they react with air and become **acidic**. When rainwater washes over these rocks, it becomes acidic, too. This pollutes the rivers and streams it flows into.

When metal, soil, or other waste runs off land at mines like this, it can pollute vital water supplies.

{case study}
Mekong River

The Mekong is the largest river in South-east Asia. As it flows 4,800 kilometres (3,000 miles) from its **source** in Tibet to its **delta** in Vietnam, it passes through six countries. It flows first through China. People living in the other five countries downstream believe that activities in China are changing the amount of river water they have.

Trickling water

The water in the lower reaches of the Mekong is far shallower today than it was in the past. Occasionally it is little more than a trickle. This is partly due to low rainfall in recent years. It is partly due to the increase in the population that lives along the river and uses its waters. Many people believe it is mostly due to huge **dams** on the Mekong in China. These were built to remove river water for **hydroelectric power** and **irrigation**.

China already has two large dams on the Mekong. In this picture a third dam is being built. There are plans to build six more dams along this river in the future.

Increasing problems

The reduction in the flow of water downstream is changing the lives of many people. In Burma, Laos, Cambodia, Thailand, and Vietnam, people rely on the Mekong for drinking water, food, and transport. Most of the rice grown in Cambodia relies on the water, **sediment**, and **nutrients** brought by the regular **floods** along the Mekong. If more dams are built, there will be fewer floods and less rice grown. The number of fish in the river is declining, which is bad news for Mekong fishermen. As the river gets shallower, sand and mud banks appear along its sides. These can be hazardous for fishing boats and ferries.

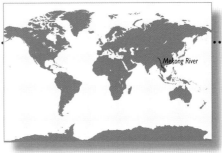

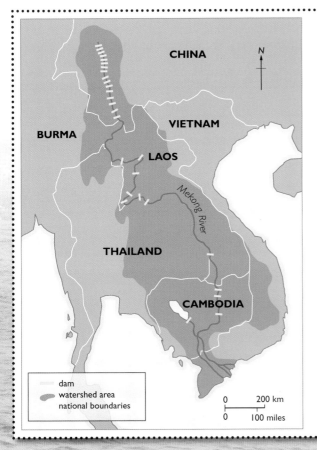

*In this map the white lines show the borders between the different countries. The dark green area is the **watershed**, the area of land that drains into the river. The yellow lines across the river show where countries have built small dams and other constructions to collect or divert water for their people.*

{water disasters}

Flooding and **drought** are water disasters that can happen almost anywhere in the world. With flooding the problem is that an area gets too much water too quickly. In a drought the problem is that a place gets too little water.

Drought

A drought happens when a place has little or no rain for so long that the lives of people, plants, and animals are badly affected. Droughts are worst in countries with a hot, dry **climate**, such as Somalia in Africa. In these places droughts can drag on for years.

Drought causes terrible misery in poorer, **less-developed countries**. Not only do people go thirsty, but also their food **crops** die. This means they do not have enough money to buy the water or food they need. In some places, farmers are being encouraged to prepare for drought by planting crops that can survive on very little water.

Flooding

People whose towns and villages are flooded face the opposite problem. There is too much water. When storms bring heavy rains, rivers and lakes may overflow their banks. The floodwater moves over land with incredible force and speed. It can wash away cars, damage buildings, ruin crops, bury entire towns under mud, and endanger lives. Even when the flood has stopped raging, the water it leaves behind is of no use to people. The floodwater is **polluted** with mud, **sewage**, and other waste.

The effects of global warming

Flooding and drought are natural disasters but they are made worse by the effects of **global warming**. The increase in the world's temperatures is affecting climates. In future there will be more cases of extreme rainfall leading to more floods. The heat will make water **evaporate** faster from the land, leading to more droughts. Not only that, but global warming is gradually melting polar ice. The water released is flowing into the sea and raising sea levels around the world's coasts.

Too much water: In a flood, water can cover and destroy roads, buildings, and fields of crops. Floodwater is polluted by dirt and sewage and can spread disease.

Too little water: In a drought, valuable farm crops wilt, turn brown and die because of a lack of water. Without food plants, people and animals can starve.

{case study}
drought in Australia

Australia is one of the driest regions on Earth. **Droughts** are a regular feature in this region. However, in 2002 the average temperatures reached new highs. Australia was hit by its worst drought since 1910.

What happened?

The drought affected the land, plants, animals, and people. Many wild plants died. Large areas of **crops** and **pasture** shrivelled away to nothing. In some places the only way farmers managed to keep their farm animals alive was by transporting water from elsewhere in tankers. Production of the country's main crops, such as wheat and barley, was reduced by about half. Many farmers lost their jobs or were forced to sell their farms. As plants and trees became drier there were more wild fires, which spread quickly and sometimes damaged homes.

*The first signs of drought are plants turning brown and wilting. Then, as **groundwater** supplies of water are used up, the soil starts to dry out and crack. Dusty soil blows across the land.*

Water restrictions

In Australia, water restrictions are a fact of life. The only water supply in some parts of the countryside is from tanks that fill with rainwater. Since the drought in cities such as Melbourne, there have been restrictions on washing cars and watering lawns. During the worst part of the drought, people were banned from using sprinkler systems to water gardens, and from using hosepipes to wash paved areas and windows.

Hotting up

The year 2002 was the fourth driest Australia had ever known. Daytime temperatures were warmer than average. Many of the warmest areas were also the driest and suffered the worst effects of the drought. This map shows the areas of Australia that were hotter than usual. Many scientists blamed **global warming** for the higher temperatures, although one hot year does not prove a trend. The hot weather increased **evaporation** of water from the land. It sped up the drying up of the soil and water sources. Increases of only 1 or 2 degrees may not sound much, but they make a big difference to water supplies and water use.

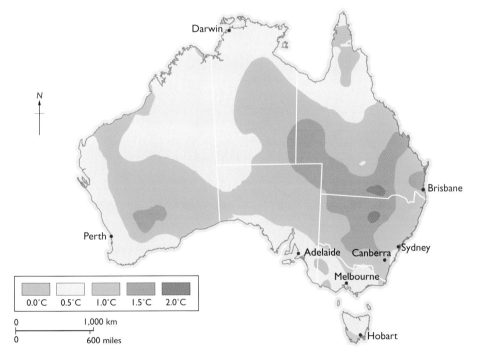

This map of Australia shows where temperatures were above average and where drought hit hardest.

{water and the natural world}

The world's freshwater isn't just a source of life for us. It is also needed to top up rivers, coastal **wetlands**, and the millions of plants and animals they shelter. When **habitats** like these are damaged or destroyed the plants and animals living in them lose their homes and often their lives too.

Changing wetlands

Wetlands are rich in wildlife and a prime example of the effects of freshwater habitat loss. Wetlands dry out when people use up **groundwater** or when **dams** remove too much water from the rivers that feed wetlands. Reeds and other wetland plants die. The animals living there may die or leave to search for a new home. Healthy wetlands are important breeding grounds for fish, birds, and many other animals. Wetland plants filter out **sediment** and dirt from **polluted** water, keeping the water fresh and clean.

*This is Coto de Donana in Spain, a vast wetland area rich in plant and animal life. These wetlands have shrunk by four-fifths because so much water has been taken for **irrigation** of strawberry fields and for tourist developments in the area.*

A matter of life and death

Pollution can also destroy freshwater habitats. **Fertilizers** run off farmland or **sewage** flows into streams that flow into lakes. These materials are full of **nutrients** that provide food for small green **algae**. The algae reproduce quickly and increase in number. They rapidly spread over the surface of the water like a slimy blanket. These gigantic masses of algae are called algal blooms.

Individual algae in a bloom live a short time and then die. **Bacteria** in the water rot the dead algae. As they do this, they use up **oxygen** dissolved in the water. Algal blooms also block light. Without light and oxygen the plants, fish, and other animals in the water die. In a lake like this the water becomes unhealthy to use. We can no longer use it as a source of fish to eat. Damaging a water system damages plants, animals, and people.

The green algae in this picture have spread and filled the water in a pond. A harmful algal bloom like this can produce toxins (poisons) that can kill plants and animals.

{animals under threat}

A wide variety of animals find food, shelter, and drinking water in rivers, lakes, and **wetlands**. Many plant and animal life cycles completely depend on freshwater. For example, frogs lay eggs in water where the young hatch and grow up before moving onto land.

Across the world

Pollution affects animals in different ways. Frogs breathe partly through their skin. If water is polluted, they cannot breathe properly. Farming chemicals called **pesticides** have washed from **crops** into lake water in Florida. They stop alligators in the lakes from breeding properly.

When people clear up pollution in rivers, more animals live there. Around 30 years ago very few river otters lived in rivers in the UK, because pollution harmed them and killed the fish they eat. Thanks to laws preventing pollution and making water cleaner, the number of otters is increasing once again.

Losing out

In the 20th century over 120 types of freshwater animals became **extinct**. Around 20 percent of the world's freshwater fish species (types) are in danger of dying out because of freshwater pollution and habitat loss.

The Amazon River dolphin is just one of many beautiful river animals in danger of extinction.

Food webs

The **food web** diagram on this page shows a network of living things that feed on each other in the River Nile. Food webs like this show us how the lives of all the plants and animals in a **habitat** are connected. If something damages one part of the web, this can seriously affect plants and animals elsewhere in the web.

For example, **fertilizers**, chemicals dumped by factories, and waste from cities have polluted parts of the River Nile. They have killed many water plants. Many other animals, including catfish, have died because there are fewer plants to eat. This in turn has meant that some Nile crocodiles and kingfishers have died because the catfish was one of the fish that they hunted for food.

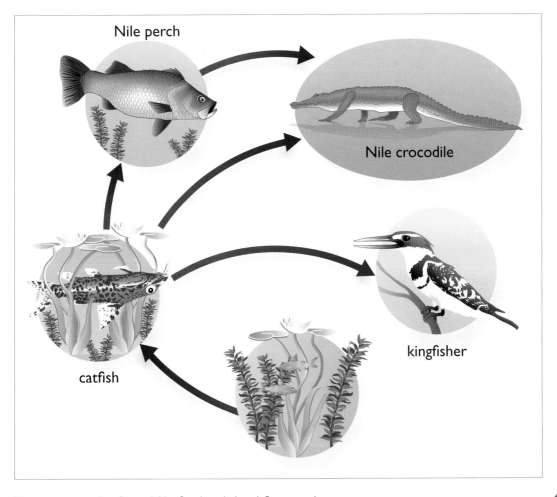

Nile perch

Nile crocodile

kingfisher

catfish

The arrows in this River Nile food web lead from a plant or animal to the animals that eat it.

{investigating water stresses}

Around the world, scientists, governments, and **conservation** groups are studying the issues of water use and **pollution** to ensure everyone will have enough water in the future.

Pollution watch

Scientists carry out tests on water supplies. They take samples of water from different river and **groundwater** sources to see if they are polluted. They work out what kinds of pollution there are. They also observe how healthy the plant and animal life around a freshwater **habitat** is. Regular checks like this mean that scientists can spot problems early and tell governments about them. Then governments can make laws to protect the river habitats, for instance by fining factories that release harmful chemicals.

Conservation and information

Many conservation organizations, like Friends of the Earth and WWF, make sure governments are doing enough to protect our freshwater supplies. They use money that people donate (give) to check up on water pollution. They organize river clean-ups, where local people get together to clear rubbish from rivers or streams that could cause serious pollution. Groups like this also inform people about the importance of using water carefully and preventing pollution.

FACT!

An ecologist is a scientist who studies the connections between different kinds of living things and their world. Ecologists help us understand that we all need to protect the natural world and freshwater sources to survive.

Cleaning up at Friar's Creek

Ecologists in Texas are preventing water pollution by creating a mini-wetland habitat. Dennis Hoffman and his team noticed that when it rained, polluted **runoff** poured into Friar's Creek. The pollution, such as oil and chemicals, washed off roads in local towns.

The ecologists looked at ways to slow down the runoff into the creek. They decided to turn the creek into a sort of **wetland**. They asked for help from local schoolchildren to dig the ground around the creek into channels. They then planted reeds and other river plants in the wet soil among the channels. The plants make the runoff move more slowly across the land. It then soaks into the soil. Pollution in the water is removed by the soil. This means the water that enters the creek is much cleaner.

Student volunteers planting wetland species at Friar's Creek.

{the future}

The world cannot increase its water supply. All we can do is change the way we use the water that we have. **Conserving** freshwater is thought to be one of the biggest challenges our world will face in the near future. Reducing the amount of water we use, **pollute**, and waste are the main ways we know of at present for solving this problem. Part of the challenge lies in education — ensuring that everyone in the world understands that water is a precious resource that is vital for the health and happiness of us all.

Reducing waste

Many countries are already working to waste less water. In some cities, lots of clean water is lost through leaky pipes. After ten years of mending pipes, the city of São Paulo in Brazil reduced its amount of wasted water by half. People are also developing ways of reusing water in buildings. Water from washing machines or sinks, for example, can be used to flush toilets. This means less clean water is wasted in toilets.

Polluted seas

About three-fifths of our planet is covered in seawater. Because the oceans are so wide and deep, people think that waste cannot pollute them. They think the problem will just dissolve or float away in the water. However, the world's ocean environment is being polluted. Some pollution comes directly from the growing number of cities along the world's coasts. Some pollution washes down rivers into the sea. Some is dumped from ships.

Can we take the salt out of seawater?

Some people believe that desalination factories, which take the salt out of seawater, might one day solve water shortages. Some people living by the world's coasts already rely on desalination factories for their freshwater. There are several problems with desalination. It is very expensive. It also creates mountains of waste salt that are difficult to get rid of.

Take action!

These are some of the ways we can all make a difference, both to saving water and to keeping it pollution-free.

Save water by turning off the tap while you clean your teeth. You can save 50 litres (13 gallons) of water every time you take a shower instead of a bath.

Plant native trees and plants in your garden, because these won't require so much water to grow. Collect rainwater in a water butt for watering plants.

Never drop litter and keep water free of pollution by reducing the amount of household cleaners that your family washes down the drain. Don't pour things like leftover paint or oil down the drains.

*Around the world people are trying some unusual ways of getting water. The people of this small village in Chile use giant plastic nets to trap fog. Then, when the **water vapour** in the fog **condenses** and turns back to water, this is carried in pipes to the village.*

{further resources}

Books

Taking Action: WWF, Louise Spilsbury (Heinemann Library, 2000)

Discover Nature in Wetlands: Things to Know and Things to Do, E. Lawlor and P. Archer (Stackpole Books, 2000)

River Food Chains, Emma Lynch (Heinemann Library, 2004)

Websites

You can explore the Internet to find out more about water. Websites can change, so if the links below no longer work use a reliable search engine.

Why not try some of the activities, games, and puzzles in the kids' section of www.groundwater.org/.

The website of WWF has information about wetlands at risk at www.panda.org.

Learn more about WaterAid's work in helping people in **less-developed countries** get clean water at www.wateraid.org.

{glossary}

acidic something that has strong chemicals in it that can burn or damage things

acid rain rainwater that has been polluted by chemicals in the air, making it acidic and damaging to wildlife

algae plant-like living thing which can be small as in the alga that floats on ponds or large as seaweed

aquifer pool of water under the ground that can be pumped up through a well

bacteria tiny living things found everywhere, in air, water, soils, and food. Some bacteria are good for us; others can cause disease

climate usual weather pattern in an area

condensation when water turns from a gas (water vapour) to a liquid

conservation protecting and saving wildlife and parts of the natural world such as rivers

crop plant grown to sell as food or other products, such as rice and cotton

dam barrier built across a river to stop its normal flow. Dams are used to redirect and store water in a reservoir.

delta triangular area of land where slow-moving river water meets the sea

deposit leave behind

drought long period of time without rain or with too little rain

erosion wearing away of rock or soil, for example by wind or water

estuary part of a river where it widens and meets the sea

evaporate change from a liquid into a gas; for example, water evaporates to form water vapour

extinct when a kind of living thing has died out completely

fertilizers chemical powders, sprays, or liquids used to improve soil and help plants grow

flood when water overflows its banks and washes onto dry areas of land

food web diagram that shows what eats what in a habitat. There are many connections in a food web, so the diagram looks rather like a spider's web!

germ tiny living thing that can cause disease

global warming rise in temperatures across the world, caused by the greenhouse effect (blanket of gases in the air that are trapping heat)

groundwater water found under the ground's surface, in cracks, or between bits of sand, soil, and gravel

habitat natural home of a group of plants and animals

hydroelectric power electricity made using the energy of moving water

irrigation supplying water for crops, parks, golf courses, and lawns through channels

less-developed country country that is less industrialized, such as many countries in Africa, Asia, Latin America and the Caribbean, and Oceania

monsoon rainy season in parts of Asia, Africa, and elsewhere

more-developed country wealthier, more industrialized country, such as countries in Europe, the USA, Canada, Australia, New Zealand, and Japan

nutrient chemical that plants and animals need to grow and survive

oxygen gas in the atmosphere that living things need to breathe in order to live

pasture grass for farm animals to eat

pesticides chemicals used to kill insects and other crop pests

pollution something that poisons or damages air, water, or land.

reservoir artificial lake for storing water

runoff water that does not become absorbed by Earth but flows across the surface of the land into a stream or lake

sanitation system of disposing of waste from people's bathrooms

sediment tiny pieces of rock and mud that often settle at the bottom of a river

sewage human waste carried away from people's homes in drains

source starting place of a river

water cycle the never-ending movement of water between the atmosphere and the Earth's surface

watershed the area of land from which rainwater or streams drain into a river

water vapour when water is a gas in the air. Clouds are made of water vapour

wetlands swamps and other damp areas of land

{index}

Titles in the *Geography Focus* series include:

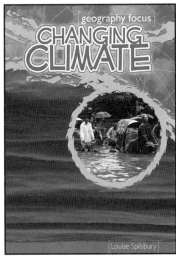

Hardback   1 74070 275 1
                978 1 74070 275 1

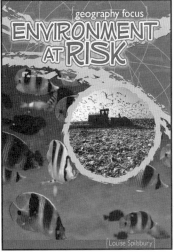

Hardback   1 74070 278 6
                978 1 74070 278 2

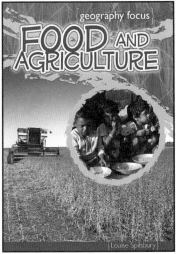

Hardback   1 74070 279 4
                978 1 74070 279 9

Hardback   1 74070 277 8
                978 1 74070 277 5

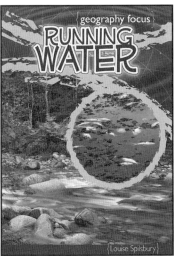

Hardback   1 74070 276 X
                978 1 74070 276 8

Hardback   1 74070 274 3
                978 1 74070 274 4

Find out about the other titles in this series on our website www.raintreepublishers.co.uk

DUDLEY SCHOOLS LIBRARY
AND INFORMATION SERVICE

Schools Library and Information Services

S0000675252